THE TRUTH IS HERE

JACK MITCHELL

RB

Rossendale Books

Published by Lulu Enterprises Inc.

3101 Hillsborough Street

Suite 210

Raleigh, NC 27607-5436

United States of America

Published in paperback 2015

Copyright Jack Mitchell © 2015

ISBN: 978-1-326-39195-9

CONTENTS

1. ALIENS, THE BEGINNING

Let me begin, by asking you to answer a simple question, with yes or no as your answer, none of this could be, maybe, I don't know, couldn't give a toss really, have a look at the question and in particular the way it is worded, here is the question, do you think in this vast universe of ours, that we are the only intelligent life, or are we all alone, that's it, have a think, and answer yes or no only! Ok, thought about it, well your answer should be no.

Of course we're not alone, we've been having visitors from outer space for thousands of years.

Governments, from all over the world have covered up alien sightings, or played them down as weather balloons, or a trickery of light and clouds when photographed, or a fault of the camera.

Why they wanted to cover them up, I don't know.

A UFO as we know them

But these visitors, in their flying saucers, as we call them, or U.F.Os unidentified flying objects, have to my mind, never attempted to land or do us harm, so the cover up is a mystery, and don't forget also, these flying saucers have been seen and reported, even filmed by high ranking forces personnel, that is colonels in the army, wing commanders in the airforce, fighter pilots, civilian aircraft, as well as the general public.

So, what propels these small crafts, well it certainly isn't a 1500 ford engine. They can leave our fastest fighter planes (which can achieve speeds of 1500 miles per hour) for dead.

When filmed, one moment they are stationary, the next moment they have vanished before our very eyes with terrific acceleration, just what kind of unit produces this kind of speed, no one knows, the only conclusion I can come up with, they could be powered by the sun.

Well let's face it, we are now using, and harnessing power from the sun in these solar panels, that people are having installed to produce electricity.

That is just my opinion, some how I can't see an electric motor driving these crafts, they may be using the sun to energise some form of unit we cannot envisage.

Why do they visit, why don't they land, where do they come from, who is their leader, these are questions at the moment we cannot answer.

A guy once asked me in a pub, why don't they make themselves known, and I replied, perhaps H. G. WELLS had it right in his book THE WAR OF THE WORLDS, when the aliens opened the door, our germ warfare killed them.

But what of the Roswell Incident!!, in 1947, in the USA, this is where a flying saucer has supposedly gone out of control and crashed in the desert, and blew up into thousands of pieces, the American army were quickly on the scene, and claimed they found some metal, they could bend, yet could not cut it.

There was no mention of finding a power unit (engine) because you can bet, by now they would have copied it, but guess what!! With all these bits and pieces scattered all over the place, the yanks reckon there were two alien bodies, one was blown to bits, the other was dead, but in complete form, but when you look at the picture of the alien who was not blown to bits, it looks like a blow up doll? Very strange don't you think, one body not blown up, and to me, it looks to human like, the only description we've got of aliens, are from drawings discovered in caves in south America, and from people who claimed they have been abducted.

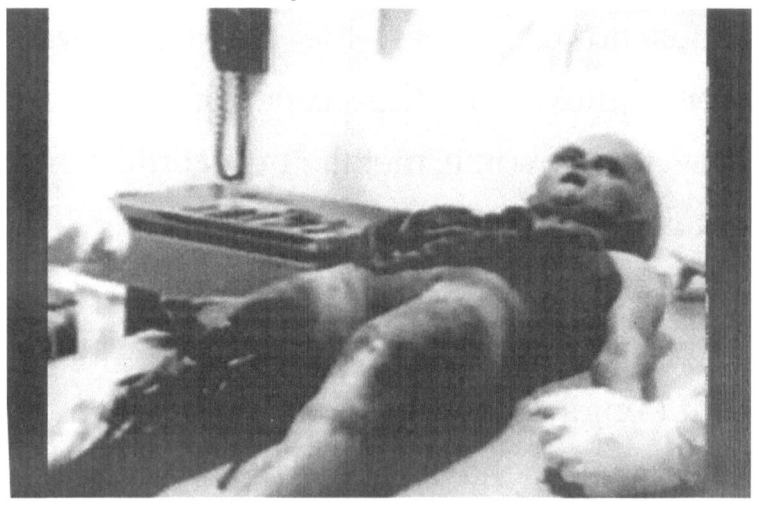

The Roswell body looks more like
a blown up doll

Sceptics, are now believing it never happened, neither did the moon landing, some think it was a distraction, because the world governments were still angry at the Americans for dropping the two bombs on Japan.

Also, a lot of sceptics are thinking why America, why didn't this alien craft crash in Europe, Russia, the middle east, or even the UK, as for the roswell incident, I'm not going any further on that subject, there are enough books on that issue in print, if you wish to find out more.

What really surprises me is, we have an international space station that's been built over the years, its main job is to look for alien visitors, and any radio messages that maybe sent, this station can see way beyond anything we can see from the ground, it would see these small crafts coming, and indeed track them back to which direction they are heading for, but they of all people have not reported seeing such objects, while people in aircrafts or on the ground are still reporting sightings, strange that!, why the deadly silence.

Also, if these aliens were of a violent nature, they would have destroyed the international space station during its construction, but it still remains a mystery why they keep buzzing us?

2. HOW DID WE GET HERE?

At this point, I must tell you I believe in god.

So during this chapter, let's think of god as a supreme scientist, who created living life that is us, human beings, he could also have created (and I don't see why not) elephants, bison, cows. Horses etc.

I know that stagnant water will create very small insects from the bacteria that forms in the water, but humans and large animals, no!

I don't believe Darwin's theory of evolution, we were taught in school that god made us, and I believe that.

Darwin claims we evolved from apes, but there are still apes around and they can't swim, so where did they come from?

There are plenty of places around the world where apes don't live, but there are humans, and have been since time began, the likes of the UK, America and Europe plus other countries.

Still, his book made him a lot of money, it is claimed he made £100.000, and at that time was an enormous amount of money, probably £10 million on today's standard, still it was good luck to him.

There are lots of ancient drawings, discovered in caves and on rocks by archaeologists all around the world, and quite a lot of these drawings show alien visitors and human beings.

There is one particular drawing that shows a face of a human Being, that appears to be looking out of a window of a spacecraft. And it is seen, wearing a helmet with a visor, to see, the same sort or very similar to the ones used today by our own astronauts when they venture into space.

Back and foreground - humans, centre - aliens, circle - UFO and alien leaving craft

Well think about that for a moment, if we need a space suit to go into space, we would definitely need one to be brought here.

Is this an alien?

Some archaeologists think it is a drawing of an alien, wrong, it is too human like, and no one has seen an alien, the only evidence we've got of what aliens look like, is also found in these same drawings, on cavern walls, and they are shown to look like the little green men, as we have become to know them by, and don't forget these drawings were left by our ancestors.

I don't know what you think, but there has got to be a way, how we came about, and I am standing by my theory that we were delivered here.

God must have seen this planet, or even visited it, and with its vegetation and oxygen, thought I will create life that can live here in these conditions, all sorts of animals and creatures, he could have also planted additional trees, like banana, rubber, cocoa, etc, and of course bushes and small plants.

I mention small plants on purpose, because there is an abundance of them which are herbs, and I do believe there is an herbal plant to cure all of our ailments; it is up to the medical scientists to find or discover them.

There is one well known plant, the cannabis plant, this small hemp plant has proved itself to be the cure for arthritis, some doctors agree it works, others are sceptical at best, to be fair the outcome is about 50/50, why some governments are against I don't know, they have obviously got their reasons.

But it's a fact, some pharmaceutical companies have already produced a cannabis tablet ready for distribution when they get the go ahead from who ever is in power.

So what scientists need to do, is spend more time experimenting with these little beauties, and I'm sure they would find an herb for each and every one of our ailments;.

Getting back to how we got here, it say's in the bible, god created adam and eve, and they had two sons, cain and abel, this simply means, god created man and woman and they could breed from each other, we didn't come from adam and eve how could we, no we were brought here, so how did it happen.

We would need to be brought here in equal numbers of men and women, looking on the internet, I discovered there are eight different blood groups, A-B-AB-O four of these are positive + and four are negative.
So lets say we were brought here in groups of eight, four women with different

positives, and four men with different negatives, I know we can breed with different positives or negatives and they can be safe, but the same blood group in man and woman can produce abnormalities, we could have been brought in much larger groups of course, and would have to be of breeding age, say 18 to 20 years old.

God, or his helpers, and no doubt he had help setting up life on earth, would have to show us how to breed, although I think mother nature would have taken over on it's own, then show the women how to give birth, and what we could eat and drink. And which animals we could kill and eat.

Before moving on, have you ever thought to how marvellous our body construction is, we have heart, lungs, kidneys, liver and limbs, all of which do an important job in keeping us alive from day to day.

But one of the best and most mysterious organs is our brains, as well as controlling what we say and do, it also has a memory bank, how great is that, and that is why, we never forget anything, well anything of importance.

Now getting back to us being delivered here, we were obviously delivered to many different parts of the world, and after being shown the basis of survival we were left on our own, to progress to what we are today.

Talking of today, if you were to sit down and look around you, what do you see, I'll tell you what you see, a TV , HI-FI, CARPETS, WALLPAPER, and clothes you are wearing, then look out the window and what do you see, a CAR parked on your driveway, a train in the distance, a aeroplane in the sky, that's how we have progressed, but I guess, you never thought were all things came from, Well I'll tell you where!

They all came from out of the earth, that's right, out of the earth, it doesn't matter which way you look at it, everything came from the earth, because the earth itself is loaded with minerals, well just think about it, we have coal, oil, gas, iron, tin, copper and many more things we have mined for, and mixing and fusing these things together, have given us what we see and feel, now isn't that truly marvellous, amazing.

As well as being brought here in groups, we could have also been brought here in intervals, say 5 or 10 years apart, I say this because some countries were way in front of others, take Greece for example, way back then in the middle east, they had proper clothing which they had learned to make, they also used colour for some clothes from some form of dye, mainly blood from animals to give a red colour.

They also had an army with weapons, wooden knives, and knew how to make wooden wheels, and were always at war with the Trojans, another country who were progressing at that time.

Then came the Egyptians another country who had come on, they also had clothing and an army, they were probably the first country to learn the art of embalming, and put their dead in tombs, their rulers at that time were buried in what we now know as the valley of the kings, some may be buried inside the pyramids, how and why they were built is a mystery, but they were built in line with three stars. Who every so often line up with the pyramids, what the significant is I don't know.

Then there's the sphinx, a mysterious statue with the body of a lion and a head of a man, what's that all about, I don't know.

Then came the Romans, they were really advanced for the time, they had armies that were divided into groups, and each group were dressed in different colours, (uniforms) they had their foot soldiers in one colour, with their spears, knives and shields, all made of metal, probably cast iron, because iron could be melted down and poured into moulds made in the sand.

They also had archers dressed in another colour, horsemen and chariot riders.

They were also well equipped with artillery, yes, they had a heavy brigade who used giant catapults to hurl stones or a big boulder to smash walls down.
They came from Italy through Spain, France and conquered all of Europe as we now know it by.

But back in their homeland, they were very good architects, who had built palaces with hot air heating, and heated swimming pools, they built amphitheatres for entertainment, and of course the famous colosseum, where the enemy were forced to fight lions with just a knife, or fight someone else from their own country to the death.

But after conquering Europe, they came to a strip of water now known as the English Channel, they crossed in their giant rowing boats, which were powered by slaves who were forced to row these boats, often being whipped to make the boat go faster.

They then landed on British soil, what do you think we were doing, I'll tell you what, we were dressed in loin cloth, living in mud huts and hunting wild boar with wooden spears.

I would have thought we offered no resistance to the Romans, how could we, we had no equipment for a fight, and must have given up very quickly.

But the Romans were very good to us, they showed us how to build houses out of sandstone, put bridges over rivers, instead of sitting on a log and paddling, how to build roads, and most importantly build boats and sailing ships.

When they left we were a better nation, we were sailing ships in about 1100 AD and coming back with goods from other countries.

America was another country that lagged behind, also Australia and New Zealand, we were going really strong when Christopher Columbus discovered America in 1492, but Columbus actually landed in Newfoundland which is in Canada, but only a few miles from the north east of America.

Columbus lands at Newfoundland

As he ventured inland he came across the
American red Indians, and in the short
time he stayed with them studying their
habits, he noticed when one of them died,
whether a baby or an elderly person they
didn't bury them, but instead, placed the
body on a pedestal about 6 feet high (2
metres) with a pile of bracken underneath
to set fire to, when he asked why this was
done, he was told that their souls had less

distance to travel to get to paradise (heaven) but who told these Indians there was something up there! When all the action, that is the coming of Christ, happened some 1400 years before, and no one had discovered America till then.

Red Indians didn't bury their dead

The Italian explorer Amerigo Vespucci discovered south America in 1499 well after Columbus, so they could not have found out from him.

Anyway where Vespucci landed and Columbus were thousand of miles apart, quite a mystery don't you think? America discovered 523 years ago as I write, my how that country has developed in such a short time, but the same can be said of Australia and New Zealand, they have had a lot of help from settlers from other countries.

Talking of Vespucci, when he landed in south America and ventured inland he came across the famous Inca temple, the mystery of this temple is, it has four sides, with steps on each side and when added all together represent the days in a year, the top platform counts as a leap year, and the four sides count as the weeks in a month, the temple is thousands of years old, and has been rebuilt about four or five times, the original was built out of timber.

So who told the Incas this know how, they hadn't got the knowledge to work it out, they must have been told?

3. CANCER: WILL WE FIND A CURE?

This is without a doubt the worst word in the English language, or any other language for that matter, it strikes at any age, old, middle age, and even infants and babies, with infants and babies it makes our blood boil, and we always say, "why does god allow this to happen", well to be honest it has nothing to do with god, he's left us alone, for us to find out the cure for all our ailments, and he has left us well supplied with the cures out there for us to find.

I know it is very sad indeed, when you find out a loved one has got this disease, but if they're in their eighties, we say, " well they've had a good innings" but that's not the point, cancer has been around long enough now, and we should have found a cure by now.

So lets take a look at why it happens, and this is what I believe, it's got nothing at all to do with god, it's in our genetic make up,

Putting it simply, there are happy families in this world, and some not quite so happy, why is this, it's because some families have what is known as a black sheep, a rogue, one who don't like the way the family is run, you know the sort, you are wrong and they are right, and in their little weird brain they truly believe this, and they disrupt the family.

According to the bible, god had this very thing happen to him, a black sheep angel, a rogue, who thought gods way was wrong and his way was right, but god was having none of it, and stamped him out and trod on him, and sent him to a place called hell, and said you rule that, his name was Lucifer, Satan, the devil, call him what you will, but that's where all bad people go.

You may wonder by now, what's all this got to do with cancer, let me explain, in the 1950s, there were headlines in all the national newspapers that some silly professor or scientists claimed smoking causes lung and breast cancer, everybody was shocked to hear such news, some people stopped smoking immediately, not going to kill me we heard them cry, so when people stopped smoking, the governments around the world increased the price of cigarettes and said it was to deter people from smoking, wrong, it was to make up for the amount of money they were losing, even today the UK is losing 3 billion pounds a year, and banning smoking in public houses made beer sales slump, so that was increased by the breweries and tax by the governments to make up the losses, it's become a cash cow, Now we hear something else causes cancer, this causes cancer, that causes cancer, they don't have a clue!

I was talking one day to my doctor, about a relative of mine who died of lung cancer and never smoked, he just shrugged his shoulders, as if to say don't know why that is.

I just mentioned a while back, how can infants get lung cancer when they have never smoked, it's because it's not caused by smoking and drinking, or eating the wrong stuff, it's caused by a rogue gene, a black sheep, we have a lot of good genes in our bodies, but one day the black sheep will raise it's ugly head and roam around our body and decide to rest some were and start growing in a cancerous form, it could be liver, lungs, prostate or whatever, the list is endless, some people have more than one rogue gene, it's called riddled with it. What a nasty expression that is, with cancer all over your body what chance do you have to live, answer, no chance.

I am going to conclude this episode with this, one day a few years ago, I read in the national newspapers that a professor or a medical scientist suggested that cancer was caused by a rogue gene that latches on one part of the body and grows as a cancer, but guess what! It was printed inside the newspaper, not the front page, in a small piece about 2 inches square, why do you think that was, it's because they don't want to admit they've got it wrong, and are more interested in the cash cow this generates.

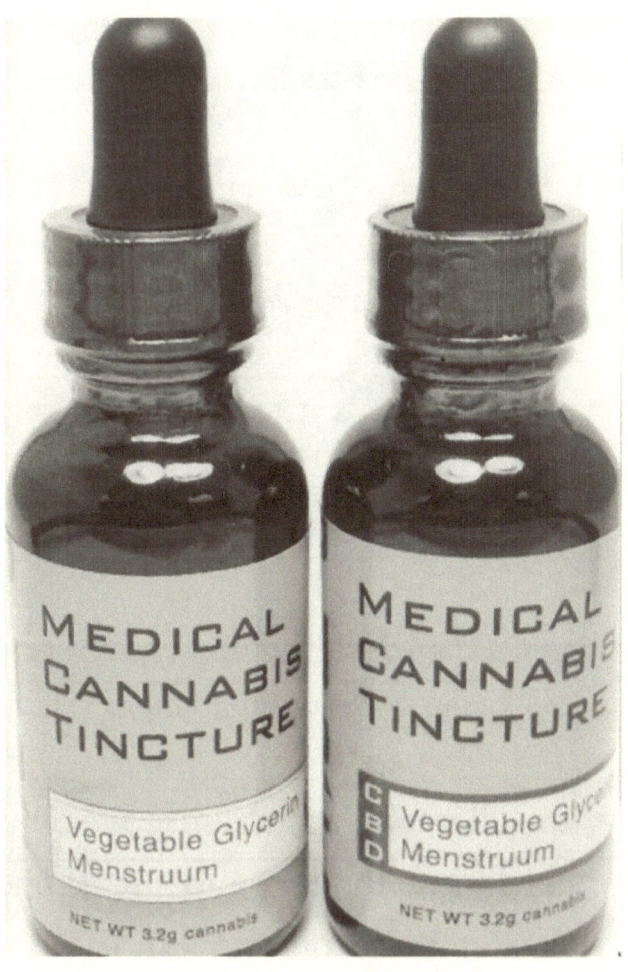

Another cancer remedy

It's claimed that this salve will remove cancer of the skin within 35 days

They are all moaning, these governments about us living longer, and are going to struggle to pay out pensions in the future, well apart from immigrants of pension age, who've never paid into the pot, they could reduce the price of cigarettes and the price of beer, lift the smoking ban in pubs, so the pensioners can drink and smoke themselves to death, if that is their wish, we are supposed to be a democratic country, but we are not, we are ruled by a dictatorial government, but they cant have it both ways can they, we should be given a choice, die as we wish to.

And finally, when I spoke about why does god allow young babies, and infants to die, it's because god has left us on our to find the cures that are here for all our ailments.

I remember way back in the 40s and early 50s, if you had pneumonia, you were a dead duck, the doctor would call the next day with the death certificate already written out, but look now theirs a cure, in and out of hospital 5 days max, so you see there is a cure out there, cancer as been around now since the 50s and we are no farther forward, I think medical scientist should concentrate more on the herbal side of products.

Stop Press: just read in the paper, a guy from Stafford England was diagnosed with bowel cancer, with no chance of survival, he was given chemotherapy which made him worse, so he stopped the chemo, and turned to a cannabis oil capsule that cured him, and he has been given the all clear, so well done to him.

So you see the point I am making about using herbal plants, it has it's great potentials, also it has been printed in the national newspapers that pharmaceutical companies have been geared up for years with a cannabis tablet, for our ailments, but we are awaiting government approval, WHY?

4. THE LIGHT AT THE END OF THE TUNNEL

You may have read in newspapers and magazines, or even seen documentaries on TV about this strange phenomenon that thousands of people have experienced, but in the main, most people say "I saw a light at the end of the tunnel, and then I woke up" that basically tells you nothing, what I am going to tell now, is the truth from my own experience of the light at the end of the tunnel.

It started when I was a 16 year old, and went to A & E, with a whitlow on my thumb, the surgeon who was examining me said "I will have to remove your thumb nail to remove the whitlow" he then proceeded by putting a mask over my nose and mouth which contained the gas ether, to send you to sleep, the last words I heard were" don't worry I won't start until you're ready" then the next thing I knew, I was flying down this tunnel posed like superman one arm forward the other arm half bent at the waist shouting whoopee, but the strange thing was, I was sitting in a dark room looking through a windowless wall inside a tunnel.

Let me explain, Imagine you're sitting in your living room and the window fitter has just removed the old window ready to fit the new one, but instead of looking outside at the scenery you are looking inside a tunnel, rather like an underground railway line, and seeing your self flying through the air, there was a yellow glow coming from the base of the tunnel, although I never saw a bulb or a lamp, and the image I saw did not have my face, but it was male, aged about seven, I don't know why that was, the only explanation I can come with, is maybe it's the age when you first have religion instruction explaining god and Jesus, but the face, perhaps that's what we all will look like when we go down the tunnel for real.

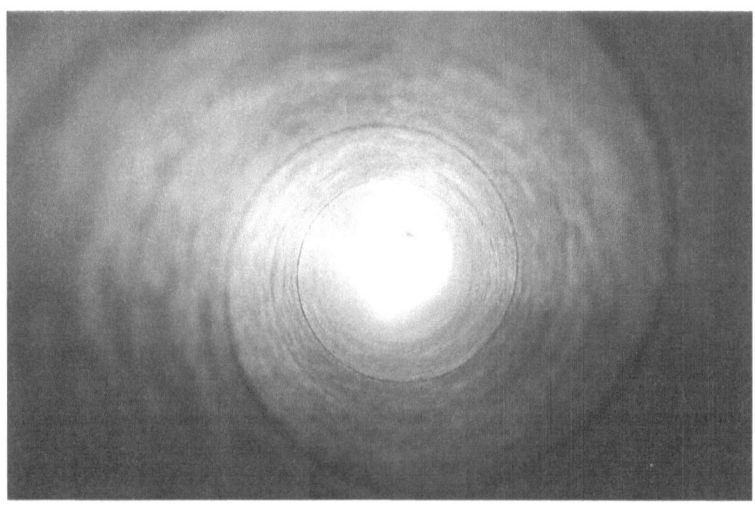

The light at the end of the tunnel

I have often wondered, whether women who experience going down the tunnel see a female image.

Any way you get the picture by now, I hope, I was flying down this tunnel, turning right, then turning left until I came to the straight bit, I say bit, it was enormous as far as the eye can see, I never saw the end, and as I was flying eventually I saw a very faint glimmer of light, it was miles away, and was as big as the point on a pin, as I got closer it got as big as the knob on a knitting needle, bearing in mind by this time the view had been changed, to me watching from behind so I could see the length of the tunnel, and that was when it happened, the brakes went on, and I stopped dead motionless in the air, and then I started to go backwards, shouting no,no I don't want to go back, I don't want to go back, then I heard a gentle voice say "where don't you want to go back to, where don't you want to go back to" it was then I realised I was coming round from the anaesthetic, and do you know what I did next, I told the doctor a deliberate lie, I said "I don't know" but on reflection I realised, I should have told him the truth.

Because doctors like to know what patients experience while under anaesthetic, and I often wonder, if the main subject is the light at the end of the tunnel.

Oops! I nearly forgot to tell you, whilst flying down the tunnel guess what! There was no wind, strange that.

5. GLOBAL WARMING

This subject really gets up my nose, and makes me mad, it's in the papers almost daily, and what makes me mad is, it's just another cash cow, that various governments throughout the world use to generate money from the tax payer, you and I.

First it was aerosol cans, that was causing global warming, so a substance in these cans was removed, but to no avail, it was still happening, so then it was petrol, and car injection systems were modified to emit less carbon, however this also didn't work, but governments through out the world were convinced it was the fuel from cars, so put up the price of fuel to make people use public transport, and leave their cars at home, this didn't work either.

I think all governments meet in secret to discuss this agenda, they send their minister of the environment to discuss what to do next, still convinced it was the petrol, they advised all road users to switch to diesel cars and vans, but after a few years they admitted this was wrong also.

The fact is, we are not causing global warming at all, it's a thing that's been happening since time began, let me explain, when I was 10 years old a few erm! Years ago, we had a teacher who I would guess was about sixty years old, yes that's right sixty, in those days you had the same teacher for all lessons in primary schools.

One day, she was giving us history and geography lessons, and she told us how the earth works, and this is what she said, quote," the earth travels around the sun at approximately 67,000 miles an hour, and from start to finish takes a year, and at the same time it is rotating at 1,040 miles an hour, and it takes a full day, 24 hours to achieve this, and while it is doing all of this, because it is a sphere it is unstable, because it also tips, but no one knows how much it tips or how often it tips," unquote.

The words global warming was not mentioned at all, this term global warming is not supported by all countries, this includes America, Spain, Italy and some other countries, but the UK and parts of Europe will not back down, and say they got it wrong, because it is a cash cow.

There is even talk now, of compensating people who were encouraged to purchase diesel cars, because scientists have now said it is making no difference at all.

Because of the tilting motion, we are now witnessing the thawing of the ice caps on one side, but in a few years time there will be a build up of ice on the other side, on both the north and the south ice caps, and this has being going on since time began, scientists seem to forget Britain once had an ice age, where we were completely covered in ice.

Can you imagine, California or Saudi Arabia in say a thousand years time being covered with ice, well with this tipping motion it is quite capable of happening, but at the moment they are basking in sunshine, but who knows, if the great thaw continues on the north and south poles, it may well reveal land, which eventually could become the hotter climes.

I have just read an article in a national newspaper, which says the silly scientists in our world, are now predicting that the thawing of the ice caps, is going to emit trillions of gallons of water.

And the sea will rise a thousand feet, the UK will be none existence and Europe will end up the size of the UK, OK I made this last bit up, but you get the point, scientists are always coming up with stupid figures that are scaremongering, but I've just told you the fact, all the water that thaws will go back to the other side of these caps, and will build up as ice, and this has being going on since time began, when will they ever learn.

As the earth tips, the north and south poles will always remain in their position, because they are the axis of the earth of which it spins around, also the equator which is the band around the centre of the earth will also remain were it is, as will the countries that are on the equator, they cannot be removed.

But what is happening to the oceans when the world tips, this is a major point, and concerns only the Pacific, and Atlantic Oceans.

Polar bears are losing their habitat

Depending which way the earth tips, either the Pacific ocean, is moving nearer the Atlantic ocean, or vice a versa, I would say at a guess that the earth must tip about every 70-80 or 90 years, I say this, because we are at this moment witnessing a movement, with the ice caps, but since the 30s, it may have been moving gradually, during this movement their occurs an under water current known as EL NINO, this is a warm water current that travels below the pacific ocean, and when it meets the cold water from the Atlantic ocean sends it into turmoil, making it travel back and forth, and causing trouble in it's wake, el nino is capable of producing vortexions, now the dictionary tells us that vortexions are either whirlwinds or whirlpools, and during the last war WW2, el nino was located around the Bermuda triangle, where aircraft and ships mysteriously vanished, scientists have come up with all different excuses why this has happened, with data, statistics , but they should stick to basic's , the fact is a whirlwind, rather like a tornado will pick up things , like a cow in a field, or a car, and sling it a quarter of a mile away, and that is what happened to the American fighter squadron in the last war that vanished over the Bermuda triangle, they got caught in a whirlwind that threw them off course, and made them crash into the sea.

The plane at the bottom of the sea in the Bermuda Triangle

*A boat at the bottom of the sea in
the Bermuda Triangle*

The same fate encountered with ships, if they got caught in a whirlpool, they were taken down to the bottom of the sea.

With the American fighter squadron that vanished mysteriously, it wasn't a full squadron, which normally consists of 18 – 24 planes, there were only 5 in this squadron, made up of TBF AVENGERS which were torpedo bombers, also on the same day, an American PBM MARINER flying boat aeroplane went missing searching for the 5 missing torpedo bombers, how strange is that, and the reason it's a mystery, is because when aircraft get caught in a whirlwind their radio contact goes dead, so they cannot give any last minute details of what's going on, and the same can be said of ships, when they get caught in a whirlpool, and there you have it, my theory of the Bermuda triangle, and the truth about global warming.

A whirlpool

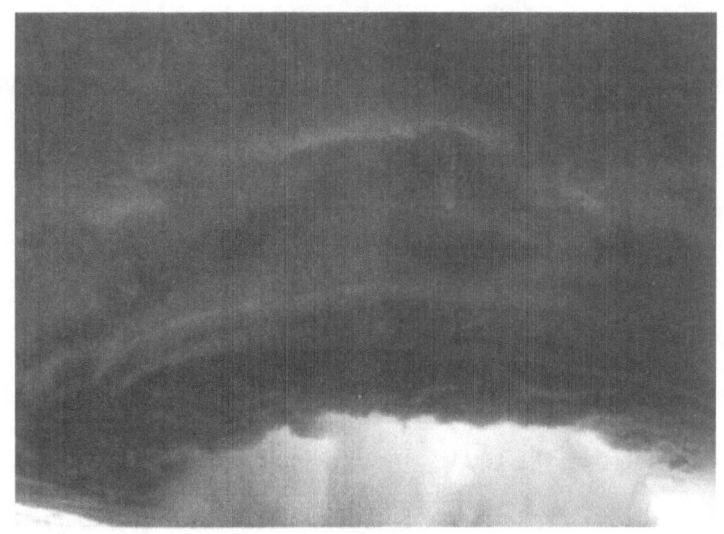

A whirlwind

6. ANALYSING THE BIBLE: THE OLD TESTAMENT

The first thing to tell you is, there is no authors name on the bible, and this is not a mystery, and will be explained as we go along, I will try to separate the myths from the facts, and that a lot of the bible is a real possibility.

This part of the book is divided into two parts, the Old Testament, and the new Testament, the new Testament is simply the life of Christ.

So lets begin with the Old Testament, there is really not to much to say about it, without printing the whole thing and trying to diagnose each part as I go along, which I am not prepared to do.

Take for example, Daniel in the lions den, legend has it, that Daniel was asked by the angels to walk into the lions den, to prove his love for god, and that god would protect him from being attacked by the lions, but there are no scrolls or parchments discovered to back this up.

This could be because, writing on hides of animal skin with blood had not been discovered, so could be a myth, don't forget we are going back a few thousand years ago, and things get exaggerated when passed down from word of mouth.

Also legend has it, that Abraham was told to offer his son Isaac as a sacrifice to god, to prove his fear of the lord, by killing him, but was stopped by an angel at the last minute, no proof could be a myth, and probably is.

Next comes the legend of David and Goliath, were a small teenager confronts a giant of a man, and kills him with a sling shot containing a stone, which hits him in the middle of the forehead, and goliath's army back off after seeing this, excuse me for saying this, but army's then only used wooden swords, they must have thought david had a new secret weapon, no proof of this, another myth I'm afraid, handed down from word of mouth.

But the one story we know for sure, is the existence of Moses, Moses was born around 1500 years before the birth of Christ It is said in the old testament, that one day Moses went to the bottom of Mount Sinai on the order from god, to pick up a covenant, well Moses didn't know what this was, (a covenant is a contract made between two or more people) and this contract was gods law, and became known as The Ten Commandments, it was an agreement between god and the people of earth.

As Moses walked to the mount, there were crowds of people watching him, and as he stood there, the crowds looked on in awe, as lightening struck the side of Mount Sinai for several minutes, then Moses went and picked up two tablets of stone containing gods rules of life, The Ten Commandments, which we all should obey to have a perfect life.

But I'm saying at this point, that the lightening part of this story is wrong, those commandments were cut out using laser, well the people in those days would not know the difference between lightening and laser.

But hang on a minute, we've got laser now, and look how good or bad it can be used, it can be very good used in surgery, indeed it is saving many lives, but used in warfare it can be deadly, it will guide bombs exactly to its target, how awesome is that.

Lightning or laser cuts
the ten commandments

The fact that we are using laser now, some 3500 years after the commandments were cut, is a sure sign of our progress.

Moses with the tablets of stone

I am not going to list all of the the commandments, just numbers, 6, 7 and 8.

Six is thou shall not murder.
Seven is thou shall not commit adultery
Eight is thou shall not steal.

Do you realise if we all obeyed just these three commandments, you wouldn't need a lock on your door, and you would be safe?

You really do have to wonder, who wrote these rules for a perfect life, and delivered them to us using laser.

But in life all rules are there, to be broken by someone who doesn't give a damn about the consequences, take murder, it's in the papers daily, sometimes two or three a day on average, why! No death penalty.

Adultery, it happens more than murder, it was in the past blamed on men, not anymore, women now instigate it more than men, my mother always said " if there were no bad women, there would be no bad men", and stealing is rife, you have burglars, pickpockets, shoplifters, and people who steal cars to order, most of these crimes are always drugs related, why! Again no penalty.

Having said that, Moses came down Mount Sinai with two stones, with five of the rules of life on each one, but, what happened to these two tablets of stone?

We are constantly told, they are here on this earth, and they are known as the Ark of the Covenant, previously known as the covenant of the lost ark.

But why archaeologists and scientists can't agree on the date of the ark because it has not been found, but do believe it came some 1500 years before Moses, therefore the tablets won't be found on Noah's boat, because a boat would not last that long in that era.

But noahs ark, as nothing at all to do with this ark, this ark is named because the box, or chest, that houses the two tablets is known as the ark.

So, what happened to the two tablets of stone, they were placed in a wooden box made out of acacia wood, then overlaid with gold, to look like a golden chest.

But where is the ark now! Some archaeologists reckon it's in muslim countries, where excavation to search for these tablets is forbidden, ifs that's the case it's going to be a long time before they find them.

Other archaeologists reckon they've ended up in Ethiopia, but originally they were kept in the temple in Jerusalem, from when they were first put in the chest, so it's anyone's guess where they are now, but I say now, when they do eventually find this golden chest, I don't think it will end up like the Indiana Jones film, where the faces of the discoverers will just melt, more realistically they will be in for a shock, especially if they discover that the tablets were cut using laser, that surely will convince them that there is a supreme being out there, and they should go down on their knees and pray, because that is what I would do.

But finally, if I was going to look for these tablets, I think I would look towards the hanging gardens of Babylon in northern Iraq, because this is a very holy country indeed, and looking inside of caves, would be a must, because I don't think they are buried, more like hiding in the wall of a cave.

7. ANALYSING THE BIBLE: THE NEW TESTAMENT

A s explained before, this is simply, The Life Of Jesus Christ.

Before I begin, I can hear the doubters shouting there's no proof that Christ ever walked on this planet, but that's the way to cover your tracks perfectly, there may not be physical evidence, but there is a lot of parchments and scrolls discovered by archaeologists from all over the world, that says he did indeed walk on this planet.

You may have heard of the dead sea scrolls, some of these were used to create the bible, so who wrote these parchments, scrolls and documents?

Let me explain, Jesus had very close friends, who were known as the apostles, they were with him all the time, and he told them to write things down what he said, and hide them in a place where they would be discovered in years to come, and that is what happened, and they were discovered by the archaeologists.

Then there were the disciples, these were told by Jesus to go and preach his word, we have disciples today, in priests, vicars and evangelists, but Jesus also told his apostles, there are something's I will tell you, that I don't want you to write down.

So, lets go to the beginning of the life of Christ, how did the scriptures know about the beginning, when Jesus was only fourteen when he started preaching, the mother of Jesus, Mary, told them how it all began.

This is how it all began, God chose a young couple who had not been married very long to have his child, they were Joseph and Mary, one day Mary had a visitor, who said he was the angel Gabriel, placed his hand on her shoulder and said " you are now pregnant with god's child, and it will be a boy ".

Look at this in a different way, lets say the angel Gabriel was a paramedic, who gave Mary IVF, we have IVF today, where women pay to conceive at £3.500 a go, some women give up after three or four goes, but here just over 2000 years ago it was one visit, and instant success, and saying the sex of the baby would be a boy, and that is how the virgin birth came about, the word virgin means untouched by man, these women today, who go for IVF, are also having virgin births.

Towards the end of Mary's pregnancy, king Herod, decided he wanted to know how many people were living in his land, so he called everyone to register at various places in his kingdom and say how many are in your family, Joseph and Mary had to register in Bethlehem.

During this period of time, prophets were proclaiming that a new king was to be born to save the world.

The Three Kings: is that a star or a spacecraft?

After Joseph and Mary had registered, they decided to stay the night, and travel back in the morning, the good book says they knocked on many doors to stay the night, but were always told sorry no room at the inn, and they ended up in a stable.

Well I think they were told to go into a stable out of sight, because just then a star appeared brightly in the sky, I don't think it was a star, but a craft with glowing lights, people then would think, that's how a star looks like when it comes near.

Have you ever wondered, how many women died back then giving child birth, I'll bet it was pretty high, as high as 50% I would guess, if a birth had complications, the women bled to death, must have been terrible giving birth in those days.

But Mary had to give birth and survive, if Mary had a paramedic at the conception, she also had one at the birth, she could have also had a caesarean section whilst out of sight, because don't forget, Mary did not die on this planet, she was ascended into heaven just like her son Jesus, why do you think this was, well I'll tell you, it was to stop the ghouls searching for her tomb and finding out what really happened, all clever stuff don't you think?

But getting back to IVF, it's not unusual for women today to pay up to £15.000 for 5 attempts, with a success rate of only 13% which is poor on today's standards, so how marvellous back then to get it right in one, we will get there in the end, that I feel is assured.

Now after Jesus was born, rumours quickly spread that a new king was born to come and save us, King Herod found out about this, and went mad, saying all young boys up to five years old were to be murdered, either by beheading or a knife through the heart, the craft (star) which hung around for about seven days after the birth, must have picked this up through eavesdropping device and told Joseph and Mary they must flee to Egypt to be safe.

Hang on a minute, we have listening devices today, we can listen to transmitted conversations, radio and telephone, so we must be catching up.

I know Christmas cards show Joseph, and Mary on a donkey travelling through the night as a lonely couple with a baby, but this may have not been the case, they could not have been the only people escaping King Herod, they may have travelled in a caravan for safety, from robbers and bandits.

A caravan, is similar to a wild west wagon train, where people travelled in groups, to be able to defend themselves better from attacks.

Can you imagine the enormity of what King Herod said in slaughtering all boys up to five years old, some families could have had two or three boys under that age, how tragic was that.

After the death of King Herod, Joseph and Mary were going back to Jerusalem to live but decided to settle in a little town called Nazareth, and that's where Jesus grew up.

It is speculated that Jesus was two years old when they settled in Nazareth, he grew up as a normal child, playing with the neighbours children as kids do, it was not until Jesus was fourteen years old, that his mother told him what he was here for, and what he must do.

So, from fourteen to twenty he set about his tasks in life, he started preaching in the synagogues and temples, in between the local rabbi's address to the congregation, and both the people and the rabbi's were impressed by how much he knew for such a young lad. Then, he had to gather together some friends, and best mates who he could trust to write down his preachings, and the story of his life.

These trusted friends were known as the apostles, who wrote down what Jesus said on scrolls, and hid them, in a place were they would be discovered, later on in years as per, his instructions, but as with all friends, there are those who will let you down when you need them most, as will be revealed.

Jesus and the apostles, started travelling from town to town spreading the word of God, in between doing their day jobs, most men at that time, were either fishermen or carpenters, some had jobs as bakers or made clothes, they had to make a living the same as we do.

Jesus only preached three main things, the first one was, when you pray, you only pray to your father in heaven, none of this worshiping false Gods, like golden eagles, or golden idols and when you pray to your father in heaven, it will begin with "our father who art in heaven", and then he wrote down all the words to the "lords prayer", which is said by Christians the world over, the second thing that he preached, was obey the ten commandments, these are Gods law, and must be obeyed, he then wrote these down for the people to see and learn.

The third thing he preached, was the one he knew, we would have difficultly in believing, and that is, there is life after death, and he repeatedly told people this, throughout his short life, don't forget he was only 33 years old when he was put to death.

This life after death, had to be earned, by people who believed, prayed, and led a good life, would be assured a place in heaven, there are however exceptions, according to the good book, people who commit suicide, do not get to reach paradise, because if they cannot value their life on earth, they don't deserve a second chance in the after life, but there are exceptions, and that is up to Gods judgement.

But come on now, how many people, pray regular and are good, not many I can tell you, what with all the crimes these days, and all the commandments broken, we have no chance of getting to paradise, or have we? What I'm about to tell you is the truth, Jesus said" if you want to gain a place in heaven, repent of your sins, and before you die, pray to your father in heaven and ask for forgiveness for all of your sins committed on this earth" nothing could be easier, you could pray on your own, in your house if you think you haven't much time left, or in hospital, nothing could be easier to get into the after life, could it, a piece of cake. Just ask the lord to forgive you of your sins, and your guaranteed a place in heaven.

Before, during and after the life of Jesus, the middle east was full of diseases, small pox, dysentery, leprosy, scabies and most likely pneumonia, all were killers without treatment, and there were none, if you reached the age of 40, you probably looked it, and were classed as old.

But during the travels of Jesus, he started to perform miracles on people who were dying from one of these diseases, so how did he do this, was it divine intervention, if so , then I must apologise to God and ask his forgiveness for doubting it's existence, but lets try and look at this from a realistic point of view, Jesus had regular visitors from yonder, one mentioned in the bible, was when the apostles fell asleep at the foot of a mountain, and when they woke up, saw a cloud at the bottom of the mountain and heard voices, and they heard, "this is my son and I am very proud of him".

Did the cloud hide a spacecraft, was Jesus given tablets or pills to cure all these ailments, bet you never thought of that.

But look at what we have now; we have different tablets or medicines for all sorts of ailments, but what about one tablet fits all, yes, we could have this right now.

Pharmaceutical companies have the technology to blend different tablets into one, take for example, paracetamol. If you go to the doctor with flu, he will recommend this tablet although your not in pain, because it contains flu shifting ingredients, you see what I'm getting at, so people who are on three or four tablets a day, could have these mixed as one tablet.

Why has it not happened, because it is a cash cow, drugs cost as I write £8.50 per item, so a person on four a day pays £34.00.

The people I feel sorry for, are those who are working and feel a bit under the weather, and just need something to keep them working, they are already paying weekly contributions, then have to pay again, while another person unemployed gets to pay nothing.

I am pretty sure that the one tablet cures all, will arrive one day soon.

Getting back to Jesus, carrying tablets in his pockets for all these cures, the people back then would obviously think it was a miracle, and if we had a tablet that did the same, so would we.

Can you imagine going into a chemists, no doctors, and asking for body boosting tablet, that would reset your whole system, rather like a default setting, then off you go fit as a fiddle.

Hang on thou, how will we die, easy, two reasons, firstly, as with all bodily organs, while we would have power over ailments, we would not stop these organs from wearing out, are but there are transplants, this would not work, because the population is dramatically increasing, and the most popular way to die, would be by cardiac arrest. And secondly, the paragraph I have just wrote about the wonder tablet, will never happen, because we are being controlled, fact is, we have all got to die.

Lets assume Jesus did use tablets to cure people, and the people did think it was a miracle, back then.

We have miracles that happen today, for instance, if a patient goes to the doctor, and he says " I'm sorry nothing more can be done " we are devastated, then you learn, a doctor or a surgeon, somewhere else in the world is experimenting on this issue, if we take the patient there, and they are cured, we would call this a miracle, and so we should.

Along the way, Jesus performed quite a few miracles, he cured a blind man, another suffering from leprosy, and so on.
It also claims in the good book, that Jesus raised a man from the dead, his name was Lazarus, the friends and relatives of Lazarus, heard Jesus was in their village

and went to see him, to ask if he could do anything to help, Jesus showed no signs of urgency and carried doing his preaching, apparently Lazarus had been dead for four days and was lying in a tomb, when Jesus did arrive, he walked into the tomb and shouted "Lazarus wake up "and he did.

Jesus could have altered his voice, to sound like a sergeant major in the army, and gave the order, "LAZARUS WAKE UP" because in reality Lazarus could have been in a coma, and not dead at all.

Jesus raises Lazarus from the dead

Have you ever thought, how many people back then, who were in a coma assumed dead, and were either buried alive or cremated, what a terrifying thought that is, but you can bet it happened.

You may have read in newspapers, stories of people coming out of comas, some with a commentary of a football match, and when the word it's a GOAL reaches the patients brain, it triggers it into action, bringing the person out of the coma, others have used pop songs and it worked, so I bet, if you did what Jesus did and called the persons name as a command to wake up, who knows, what have you got to lose by trying, it could even work.

You may think, what I've written so far, regarding the super pill, and raising people from coma's, is absolutely crazy, but not so crazy as some people today, writing about Jesus married Mary Magdalene, (a prostitute) and having two children, I don't think so, I am quoting extracts from the bible I have at home, and nowhere does it mention such rubbish.

There's no denying, Jesus did meet Mary Magdalene, in a little town called Magdala on the on the coast of Galilee, hence the name, Mary from Magdala, as he was walking through the town, he saw a huge crowd, and wondered over to see what was going on, and saw that Mary Magdalene was about to be stoned to death for being a prostitute, they were stoned to death using two methods, either tied to a stake, or were buried up to their necks in the ground, no getting away, that's for sure, so Jesus went to the front of the crowd before the execution began, held his arms up high and shouted stop, and said to the crowd; "if any of you are free from sin, then you can cast the first stone" and the crowd pulled away, leaving Mary to go free, what Jesus meant was if you steal a toffee or a car, in Gods law, both are stealing the value of the stolen article is nothing.

When Mary Magdalene was freed, Jesus told her to go and preach his word as a penance, and stop being a prostitute, and he never saw her again until he was on trial for blaspheme.

During his tours, Jesus did other remarkable things, like the feeding of the 5000 people who followed him, it is said in the bible that two fishes and five loaves were used to feed the people, the only explanation I can come up with here is, most villages were fishing villages, and they would also have bakeries.

Another story, tells of Jesus walking on water, where he asked the apostles, who were in a boat to join him, when they got out they sank, was this divine intervention, or did Jesus walk on a causeway, for people who don't know what a causeway is, it's a piece of land, rather like a footpath, that's just below the waterline, if people were watching this from the shore line, in the distance it would appear as if someone was indeed walking on water.

We now come to the third thing that Jesus preached, the mysterious life after death, I used to get bemused at funerals, when you get a husband or wife dies after their partner, and the vicar or priest says, "joined together" this is not the case, you may well be joined together in heaven, but you won't know each other, as a married couple, because our lives are completely different in paradise, let me explain.

Jesus talks to the two men

One day, when Jesus had finished preaching in a temple, there were two men waiting to see him, to ask him a question, and one of the men said "master can we ask a question" and Jesus said " of course what is it" and the one man said " if a man marries and his wife dies, and that man marries again and his second wife dies, when the man dies which wife will he be joined together with in paradise" and Jesus replied "neither, because your life on this earth is different to your life in paradise" and he went on to explain how this worked, he said " your life here on earth, is like you being a seed, you plant a seed in the ground and up grows a beautiful flower or fruit plant, and when you look at the seed, it looks nothing at all like the lovely plant it has produced, the difference is amazing" you see, Jesus said I took your form to come here, but I won't be of this form when I get back.

So our souls, which scientists think is embedded in our brain, in the form of a chip, is the only thing that goes back to heaven, with the complete history of our life, to be judged by God the father, to see if we deserve a second life, after our death.

There are paintings depicting God the father, as looking like an older version of

Jesus, with flowing white hair, and a huge white beard, similar to the picture painted on the ceiling of the Sistine Chapel by Michelangelo, but this is not true, when Jesus said "no one knows what God the father looks like" then told the two men, I took your form to come here.

Even the famous French philosopher Nostradamus, who predicted many accurate things that would happen in the future, said on his death bed "there is a paradise for I have seen it", so while we are not joined together, as man and wife, all our souls are joined together as one big happy family, if we make it of course.

During the travels of Jesus and the apostles, one day, they were sitting down having a bite to eat, when the apostles asked Jesus when and how will the world end, and he replied "only God the father knows the answer to that question".

We now come to the final chapter in the life of Jesus, The crucifixion, how did it all go so wrong, why was such a religious, and kind caring man, put to death this way, and how did he rise from the dead.

Jesus rides into Jerusalem on Palm Sunday

Well, it all happened a week before the crucifixion, what we now call palm Sunday, Jesus rode into Jerusalem on a donkey, and as usual there was a huge crowd waiting to here him speak, when Jesus dismounted, and started walking amongst the crowd he could hear them whispering and talking, and saying, surely with all what he knows about God, and the miracles he has performed, he must be the son of God, they were all nodding in approval and agreeing, Jesus then stepped on the podium, (probably a wooden box) and held his arms up high to silence the crowd, and the first words he said was "I AM THE SON OF GOD", that did it, there were gasps of astonishment, and an uneasy silence went through the crowd, when suddenly a voice shouted, blasphemer, how dare you stand their and proclaim that you are the son of God, the crowd started chanting blasphemer, and this quickly changed to death to the blasphemer.

Jesus knew what he was doing, so with the apostles they made a quick getaway from the baying crowd, and the last supper was arranged at a house that evening, which contained the garden of Gethsemane, the apostles and a few disciples were there along with a woman, (as drawn by Leonardo da Vinci) the last supper, however the woman was not Mary Magdalene, but Mary, the mother of Jesus, well if you were going to have a last meal before you die, you would certainly invite your mother surely.

During the last supper, Jesus said to Judas " you will betray me for a bag of silver", no not me replied Judas, he also said to peter you will betray me three times, before the cock crows, no, no, never peter replied.

The Last Supper

Jesus and some of his followers went into the garden to pray, Judas was missing, by this time the crowd had formed a representative committee to go and see the local governor of the roman army, who's name was Pontius Pilate.

Pontius saw the peoples representatives and asked what was wrong, they told him they wanted Jesus crucified for blasphemy, saying he was the son of God, a very serious crime in the holy land.

But Pontius Pilate didn't know this, and thought it was laughable, just ignore him said Pilate, the man's a nutter, he's done no harm as far as I'm concerned, but the people were adamant, and insisted Jesus had to be crucified for what he had said, Pilate said "I am not crucifying this man" and washed his hands of the case, and told the people, if you want to crucify this man you will do it yourselves, however I will give you some soldiers, to arrest him and escort him to the place of execution.

But the peoples committee did not know where Jesus was, enter Judas, I know where Jesus is he said, but it will cost you 30 pieces of silver, so the committee had a whip round and raised the money, and gave it to Judas in a bag.

Pilate then, told some of his soldiers to go with Judas and arrest Jesus on behalf of the people, the soldiers didn't know what Jesus looked like, because then all the males looked pretty much the same, dressed in white robes, with long hair, beards and moustaches, so Judas said " I will kiss the man you want on the cheek" so off they went, and when they reached the garden of Gethsemane, Judas went and kissed Jesus on the cheek and the soldiers duly arrested Jesus, the people who were with the soldiers pointed at peter and said your are one of his friends, no I'm not said peter, another said yes you are, no I'm not said peter, a third person said "you are I've seen you with him" he again said "no I don't know him". Just then the cock crowed, and Peter remembered what Jesus had said to him, and ran off and cried his heart out, Judas was found the next morning hanging from a tree, with the bag of silver still in his pocket.

The soldiers arrested Jesus and took him to Pontius Pilate, who in turn handed him over to the people to crucify him, along with some soldiers to escort him to mount Calvary, (it has since been discovered, it was mount Gotha), but before the journey started the people bashed a crown of thorns on the head of Jesus, causing, has you would expect massive bleeding.

Pictures in all churches, predict Jesus carrying a cross, not true I'm afraid, Jesus was made to carry the horizontal bar, usually a thick branch of a tree, to the place of execution, where they were laid down and tied to it with rope, the nails put in the hands and feet of Jesus, was carried out by the people to cause more suffering, after being tied to the bar and lifted up, probably by six soldiers, to the vertical strut and fixed, the nails were then put in his feet.

Franco Zeffirelli, who directed the wonderful series on BBC television, Jesus of Nazareth, got the execution spot on.

Jesus was tied to the cross, as was the tradition.
The nails were put in for extra pain

People executed this way, normally die of heart failure, the time from start to death varied for each individual, but did Jesus actually die, I say this, because of what is said in the bible, it is claimed that Jesus asked for water,(would you give it or not) to grant that wish, he would suffer longer, to refuse, he would die sooner, but where would you get water from, on the top of a hill, apparently Mary his mother, who was there, had got a wet cloth and asked a soldier to lift the wet cloth up on his spear to Jesus, did this cloth contain a pill, that Jesus took to put him in a coma, giving the impression he was dead, after a while when people thought Jesus was dead, a soldier shoved a spear in into his side, no reaction, from the victim, and they were declared dead.

But hang on a minute, we can induce people into comas today, somebody critical injured in a car crash, where too much morphine would have to be administered to kill the pain, and probably the victim, we do this to save their lives.

When Jesus was cut down from the cross, it is said the sky went black, and he was taken to a tomb, where a huge boulder was rolled in position by some soldiers, there was also a soldier left to guard the tomb, probably to stop the people coming to burn the body of Jesus.

However come Easter Sunday, the stone had been rolled back, the guard was asleep on the ground, and Jesus had gone, that's what the visitors to the tomb discovered, when they went to anoint the body, as was the custom then, but when did Jesus actually go, was it on Good Friday the day of the execution, or on the Saturday? He had got to be revived quickly, I would imagine, the point I'm making here is, we can now bring people back from the dead, if caught in time, in fact, we can now make people live longer with transplants, that's how we are progressing.

But will we ever be as good as the visitors who rescued Jesus?

A few days after the resurrection of Jesus, it was time for him to go, and his final words were, "remember I am with you all the time, till the end of time", he then stepped into a beam of light coming from the sky, and left us.

Well you've heard the saying surely, beam me up Scotty, and that's how Jesus disappeared.

It is quite possible, we will board planes this way in the future.

The Ascension of Jeusus - note the beam of light

I have seen various pictures of the ascension into heaven of Jesus, always in a beam of yellow light, but all the pictures I have seen never show the other end of the light, that is to say, where the light is coming from, however one day when I was in a library, where I live, I came across a lovely picture showing the ascension into heaven, this picture must have been three to four hundred years old, I don't recall the artists, but a foot note below the picture read, note the scorch marks on the ground. I said at the beginning of this story, there is no authors name on the front of the bible, but I think there should be, don't you?

The Ascension of Mary into Heaven

8. THE END OF THE WORLD: HOW WILL IT END?

Jesus told his apostles, only God the father knows when, and how the world will end.

Have you ever wondered how the world will end, well there's one thing for sure, no one knows WHEN, it will happen, but we can have a guess, how it might happen.

To my mind, there are four possibilities.

The first one, is what Nostradamus the French apothecary, (means chemist) predicted, WW3 world wide war, this would be when all the major countries, with massive arsenals of bombs, some containing poison gases, would be at each others throats, until there was a winner, not so I'm afraid, in a scenario like that, there would be No winners, each country involved would be completely destroyed, flattened, and all the people dying in agony from poisonous gases, it would be no use saying we'll have a war, but wont use gas, because they would, and when one country uses it, the others would too.

But, this is highly unlikely because, the third world countries would not be involved, how could they, they don't possess weapons, so they in turn would rise up and take over, once this has happened the world over since time began, take the Romans, the Greeks the dictators, like Hitler, to name just three who tried to conquer the world, and look what happened to them.

The second theory is, we could endure a massive bubonic plague, which could pass to each country via the clouds, and wipe us all out, but scientists would soon then discover an antidote, so this too, is highly unlikely.

The third theory is , we could be invaded from out of space by the aliens, for what ever reason they see as fit, and wipe us all out, don't know why that has not already happened, because there are some evil countries out there, but it says in the good book, evil will rise against the good, but the good will win.

My fourth theory, and the most likely one, is this, see what you think!

The earth WILL end up exhausted, in other words, no oil, gas, coal, metal, iron, copper, zinc, etc, all completely gone, then we would start going backwards.

Just imagine for instance, your car may need a new engine, or is a write off, and needs new body panels, cant do it, because were not making anymore, no materials or metal.

There would be no more TVs or phones, no massed production of anything, like clothes, because the machinery has broken and we cant get replacement parts, you get the point I'm making, all machinery would stand idle.

But we have solar power, but that could only be used to keep us in lighting, and warm radiators, and electric cookers, until they conk out, and cannot be replaced, and people who have not got solar power, would not be able to get it.

And what happens when the solar panels stop working, not repairable, so we would indeed be on a backward trend, no electricity, or gas or clothes, we would end up in loin clothes again.

The population would decline, through lack of medicines, people would die of simple illnesses like flu, people would also die in pain, it's unthinkable, but it would happen.

Don't worry yet folks, it would take about a thousand years to finalise, from the start to the finish, and it wont be in our lifetime, never the less, it will happen, and we will end up like the red planet MARS, covered in dust, but that cannot be true, because we will still have the seasons, and the animals and the birds will still be here, grazing and flying around as if nothing had happened, bet the birds will miss the bread crumbs.

Mars, the red planet: will we end up like this?

www.ingramcontent.com/pod-product-compliance
Lightning Source LLC
Chambersburg PA
CBHW051450280526
45785CB00003B/1498